Foundation Paper 3

Business Mathematics

GW01099202

First edition 2002
Third edition January 2004

ISBN 0 7517 1484 4 (Previous ISBN 0 7517 0122 X)

British Library Cataloguing-in-Publication Data

A catalogue record for this book is available from the British Library

Published by

BPP Professional Education, Aldine House, Aldine Place, London W12 8AW

www.bpp.com

Printed in Great Britain by Ashford Colour Press

Welcome to BPP's CIMA **Passcards**.

- They **save you time**. Important topics are summarised for you.

- They incorporate **diagrams** to kick start your memory.

- They follow the overall **structure** of the BPP Study Texts, but BPP's new format CIMA **Passcards** are not just a condensed book. Each card has been separately designed for clear presentation. Topics are self contained and can be grasped visually.

- CIMA **Passcards** are still **just the right size** for pockets, briefcases and bags.

- CIMA **Passcards focus on the exam** you will be facing.

Run through the complete set of **Passcards** as often as you can during your final revision period. The day before the exam, try to go through the **Passcards** again! You will then be well on your way to passing your exams. **Good luck!**

BPP also publishes a Practice & Revision Kit and MCQ cards, which contain lots of questions for you to attempt during your final revision period.

Contents

1: Basic mathematical techniques

Topic List

Integers, fractions and decimals

Order of operations

Percentages and ratios

Roots and powers

Geometric progressions

Business Mathematics is a foundation level paper which is designed to provide you with a number of mathematical and statistical concepts and techniques that you will need as you progress through your intermediate and final level papers.

Many students do not have a mathematical background and so this chapter is intended to cover the basic mathematics that you will need for the Business Mathematics exam.

Integer

is a whole number which can be either positive or negative.

Examples

Integers = –5, –4, –3, –2, –1, 0, 1, 2, 3, 4, 5
Fractions = $\frac{1}{2}$, $\frac{1}{4}$, $\frac{19}{35}$, $\frac{10}{377}$
Decimals = 0.1, 0.25, 0.3135

Fractions and decimals

are ways of showing parts of a whole.

$$FRACTION = \frac{NUMERATOR}{DENOMINATOR}$$

Significant figures and decimal places

If the first figure to be discarded is > or = to five, then add one to the previous figure. Otherwise the previous figure is unchanged.

49.28723 → Correct to four significant figures = 49.29

→ Correct to four decimal places = 49.2872

The reciprocal of a number is just 1 divided by that number

Brackets are commonly used to indicate which parts of a mathematical expression should be grouped together, and calculated before other parts. Brackets indicate a priority or order in which calculations should be made.

1 Do things in brackets, before doing things outside them

2 Subject to rule 1, do things in the following order

  (a) Powers and roots
  (b) Multiplications and divisions
  (c) Additions and subtractions } work from left to right

Negative number rules
■ $-p + q = q - p$ ■ $-p/_{-q} = p/_q$
■ $q - (-p) = q + p$ ■ $-p/_q = -p/_q$
■ $-p \times -q = pq$

Extra symbols

> greater than	< less than	$\neq$ is not equal to
$\geq$ greater than or equal to	$\leq$ less than or equal to	

Percentages

indicate the relative size or proportion of items, rather than their absolute value.

Percentage ← fraction/decimal

← divide by 100%

eg $40\% = \dfrac{40\%}{100\%} = \dfrac{4}{10} = \dfrac{2}{5} = 0.4$

Fraction/decimal ← percentage

← multiply by 100%

eg $\dfrac{3}{5} = \dfrac{3 \times 100\%}{5} = 60\%$

Proportions

mean writing a percentage as a proportion of 1 (that is, as a decimal).

Example

1 man in a group of 5 people.

Fraction = $^1/_5$

Percentage = 20%

Proportion = 0.2

Ratios

show the quantitative relationship between two or more items.

Example

Sally and Jim want to share £100 in the ratio 3:2. How much will each receive?

Number of parts = 3 + 2 = 5

Value of each part = $£100/_5$ = £20

Sally's share = 3 × £20 = £60

Jim's share = 2 × £20 = £40

The nth root of a number is a value which, when multiplied by itself (n-1) times equals the original number.

Square root

of a number is a value which when multiplied by itself equals the original number.

$$\sqrt{9} = 3, \text{ since } 3 \times 3 = 9$$

Cube root

of a number is the value which, when multiplied by itself twice equals the original number.

$$\sqrt[3]{64} = 4, \text{ since } 4 \times 4 \times 4 = 64$$

Powers work the other way round to roots.

$2^6 = 2 \times 2 \times 2 \times 2 \times 2 \times 2 = 64$

$3^4 = 3 \times 3 \times 3 \times 3 = 81$

Rules

- $2^x \times 2^y = 2^{x+y}$
- $2^x \div 2^y = 2^{x-y}$
- $(2^x)^y = 2^{x \times y} = 2^{xy}$
- $x^0 = 1$

- $x^1 = x$
- $1^x = 1$
- $2^{-x} = 1/2^x$
- $(1\frac{1}{2})^x = (3/2)^x = 3^x/2^x$

A geometric progression is a sequence of numbers in which there is a common ratio between adjacent terms.

Algebraic representation of a geometric progression

$$A, AR, AR^2, AR^3, AR^4, ..., AR^{n-1}$$

where   A = first term
R = common ratio
n = number of terms

Formula for sum of a geometric progression, $S = \dfrac{A(R^{n-1})}{R-1}$

FORMULA NOT PROVIDED IN THE EXAM – LEARN!

You are unlikely to encounter a whole question based on basic mathematical techniques – but you will find that many questions draw on these skills.

2: Formulae and equations

Variables are used to build up useful formulae. If we then put in values for the variables, we can obtain a value for something we are interested in. For example:

Profit = revenue − costs
Revenue = selling price × units sold
∴ Profit = (selling price × units sold) − costs

or $x = p \times u - c$
where $x = profit$ $u = units\ sold$
         $p = selling\ price$ $c = cost$

A linear equation has the general form y = a + bx

y = dependent variable
x = independent variable
a = constant (fixed amount)
b = constant (coefficient of x)

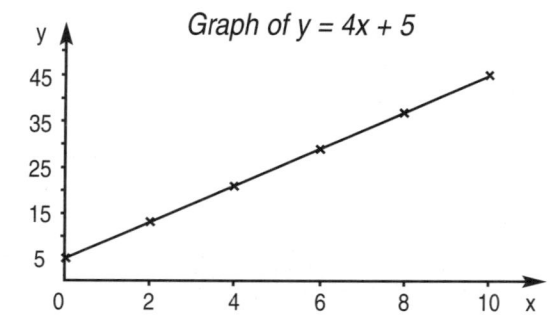

Graph of y = 4x + 5

Intercept

is the point at which a straight line crosses the y axis.

In the graph of $y = 4x + 5$, the intercept is 5.

Gradient

of the graph of a linear equation is $(y_2 - y_1) \div (x_2 - x_1)$ where (x_1, y_1) and (x_2, y_x) are two points on the straight line.

In the graph of $y = 4x + 5$, the gradient is 4.

Simultaneous linear equations are two or more equations which are satisfied by the same variable values. To find the values of unknown variables, you need as many equations as there are unknowns.

Example

$$y = 6x + 32 \qquad (1)$$
$$2y = 2x + 144 \qquad (2)$$
$$2y = 12x + 64 \qquad (3) \quad ((1) \times (2))$$
$$0 = 10x - 80 \qquad (3) - (2)$$
$$10x = 80$$
$$x = 80/10 = 8$$

If $x = 8$,
$$y = (6 \times 8) + 32 = 48 + 32 = 80$$

Graphical solution: plot equations on one graph and find their intersection point.

2: Formulae and equations

Non-linear equations are those in which one variable varies with the nth power of another where $n > 1$. They can be expressed in the form $y = ax^n + bx^{n-1} + cx^{n-2}... + constant$.

The graph of a linear equation is a straight line. The graph of a non-linear equation is not.

Quadratic equation

is a type of non-linear equation in which one variable varies with the square of the other variable (it may also include a term involving the first power of the other variable).

General form: $y = ax^2 + bx + c$

Two solutions or 'roots of the equation'

$$= \frac{-b \pm \sqrt{b^2 - 4ac}}{2a}$$

Features

- c = value of y at intercept
- a = shape of graph
- $a > 0$ = ditch-shaped with minimum point
- $a < 0$ = bell-shaped with maximum point

Graph of $y = ax^2 + bx + c$ ■

■ known as a
parabola

Note that some quadratic equations have only
one root, eg $x^2 + 2x + 1 = 0$

Notes

3: Accuracy and approximation

Approximation arises for two main reasons. It is often not possible to obtain an accurate value for a large number (town population) and some figures may only be easily measurable to the nearest whole number (car speeds). In other situations, it may not be necessary or desirable to express data as accurately as they can be measured. In such circumstances, numbers are rounded.

There are three main methods of rounding. We can illustrate rounding using the figure 18,600.

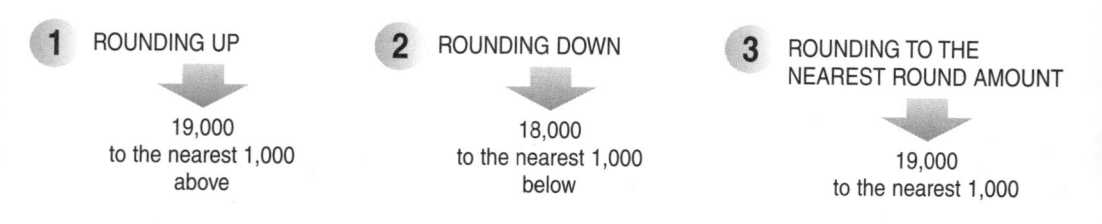

1 ROUNDING UP

19,000
to the nearest 1,000
above

2 ROUNDING DOWN

18,000
to the nearest 1,000
below

3 ROUNDING TO THE NEAREST ROUND AMOUNT

19,000
to the nearest 1,000

In rounding to the nearest unit, a value ending in 0.5 is usually rounded up.
Therefore 3.5 to the nearest unit would be 4.

Spurious accuracy arises when a statistic gives the impression that it is more accurate than it really is.

Maximum absolute error is expressed as $a \pm b$

Maximum relative error = $\dfrac{\text{maximum absolute error}}{\text{estimate}} \times 100\%$

Example

The number of pupils in a school is said to be 300 (the estimate).

Rounding	True value between	Max absolute error	Max relative error
Up to the nearest 10 (W1)	291 – 300	9	3%
Down to the nearest 10 (W2)	300 – 309	9	3%
To nearest 10 (W3)	295 – 304	5	1.67%

Workings
(1) Maximum absolute error = $300 - 291 = 9$ Maximum relative error = $\frac{9}{300} \times 100\% = 3\%$

(2) Maximum absolute error = $309 - 300 = 9$ Maximum relative error = $\frac{9}{300} \times 100\% = 3\%$

(3) Maximum absolute error = $300 - 295 = 5$ Maximum relative error = $\frac{5}{300} \times 100\% = 1.67\%$

3: Accuracy and approximation

Addition/subtraction

If two or more rounded or approximate numbers are added or subtracted, the maximum absolute error = the sum of the individual maximum absolute errors.

Example

Total cost of product V
= £10 Material A (to nearest £)
  £100 Material B (to nearest £10)

Maximum absolute error
= £0.50 + £5.00 = £5.50

Maximum relative error
= $\frac{£5.50}{£110*}$ × 100% = 5%

*£10 + £100 = £110

Multiplication/division

If two or more rounded or approximate numbers are multiplied or divided, the approximate maximum relative error in the result = the sum of the individual maximum relative errors.

Example

SV Ltd plans to sell 1,000 units (to the nearest 100 units) at £100 (to nearest £10) per unit.

Approximate maximum relative error
(50/1,000 × 100%) + (£5/£100 × 100%) = 5% + 5% = 10%

Approximate maximum absolute error
10% × (1,000 × £100) = £10,000

Actual maximum absolute error
(1,049 × £104) − (£1,000 × £100) = £9,096

4: The collection of data

Topic List

Data and information

Types of data

Primary data

Secondary data

Sampling methods

Data is a 'scientific' term for facts, figures, information and processing. Data are the raw materials for data processing. Examples of data include the following.

- *The number of tourists who visit Hong Kong each year*
- *The sales turnover of all restaurants in Exeter*

Data needs to be collected so that it can be presented in a useful form (tables, graphs) before it is analysed further.

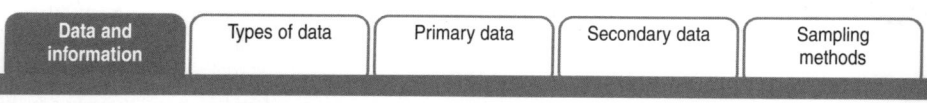

Data and information	Types of data	Primary data	Secondary data	Sampling methods

Information is data that has been processed in such a way as to be meaningful to the person who receives it. Information is anything that is communicated.

Quantitative data are data that can be measured $\longrightarrow$ variables

Qualitative data are data that cannot be measured $\longrightarrow$ attributes

Something an object either has or does not have.

Characteristics of good information

- Relevance
- Completeness
- Accuracy
- Clarity

- Confidence-inspiring
- Properly communicated
- Costs less than the value of benefits
- Manageable volume

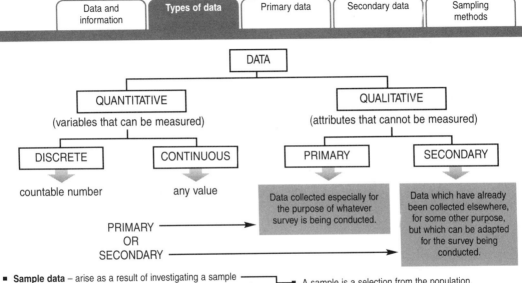

DATA

QUANTITATIVE
(variables that can be measured)

QUALITATIVE
(attributes that cannot be measured)

DISCRETE → countable number

CONTINUOUS → any value

PRIMARY
Data collected especially for the purpose of whatever survey is being conducted.

SECONDARY
Data which have already been collected elsewhere, for some other purpose, but which can be adapted for the survey being conducted.

PRIMARY
OR
SECONDARY

- **Sample data** – arise as a result of investigating a sample
- **Population data** – arise as a result of investigating a population

A sample is a selection from the population.

4: The collection of data

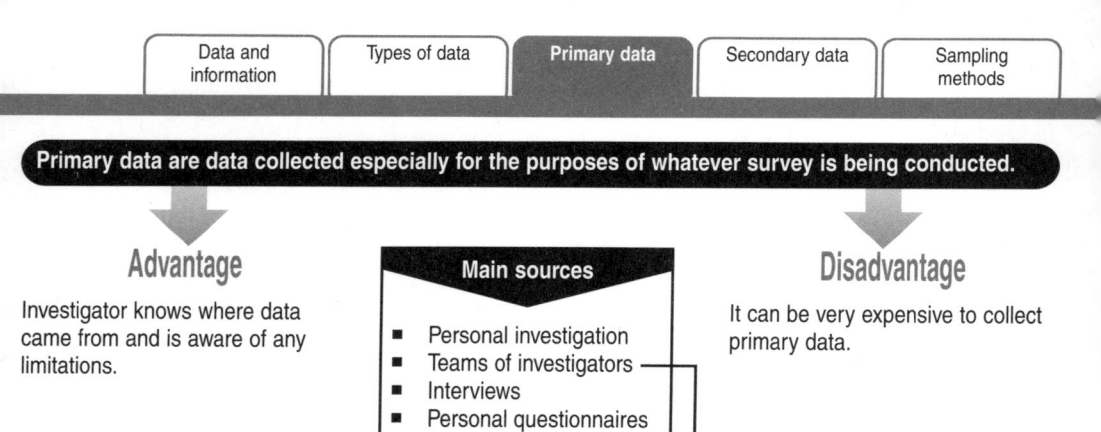

Primary data are data collected especially for the purposes of whatever survey is being conducted.

Advantage

Investigator knows where data came from and is aware of any limitations.

Primary sources of data

- Eyewitness to an event
- Document under scrutiny

Main sources

- Personal investigation
- Teams of investigators
- Interviews
- Personal questionnaires
- Telephone surveys

- Advantages include rapid response and covering a wide geographical area

Disadvantage

It can be very expensive to collect primary data.

- Surveys can be carried out by a team of investigators who collect data separately and then pool their results

Secondary data are data which have already been collected elsewhere, for some other purpose, but which can be used or adapted for the survey being conducted.

Advantage

Cheaply available.

- *Annual Abstract of Statistics*
- *Monthly Digest*
- *Financial Statistics*
- *Economic Trends*
- *Regional Trends*
- *The Blue Book*
- *The Pink Book*
- *Social Trends*

Secondary data sources

- Governments
- Banks
- Newspapers
  - *Financial Times*
  - *Wall Street Journal*
- Trade journals
- Advice bureaux
- Consultancies
- Reference books
  - Radio
  - TV
  - Teletext
  - Internet
- Libraries
- Electronic sources

Disadvantage

Investigator unaware of any limitations of the data

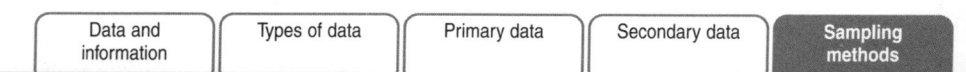
In situations where it is not possible to survey the whole population, a sample is selected. The results from the sample are used to estimate the results of the whole population.

In situations where the whole population is examined, the survey is called a **census**.

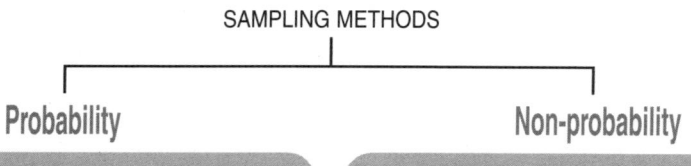

SAMPLING METHODS

Probability

A sampling method in which there is a known chance of each member of the population appearing in a the sample.

Non-probability

A sampling method in which the chance of each member of the population appearing in the sample is not known.

Probability sampling methods

- Random
- Stratified random
- Systematic
- Multistage
- Cluster

A simple random sample is a sample selected in such a way that every item in the population has an equal chance of being included

If random sampling is used it is necessary to construct a sample frame

Sampling frame characteristics

- Completeness
- Accuracy
- Adequacy
- Up-to-dateness
- Convenience
- Non-duplication

Sampling frame

is a numbered list of all items in a population.

Readily available sampling frames for the human population:

- Council Tax Register
- Electoral Register

Stratified random sampling

is a method of sampling which involves dividing the population into strata or categories. Random samples are then taken from each stratum/category.

Features

- Sample selected is representative
- Structure of sample reflects that of population
- Inferences can be made about each stratum
- Higher precision is obtainable
- Requires prior knowledge of each item in the population

Systematic sampling

is a sampling method which works by selecting every n^{th} item after a random start.

Features

- It is easy to use
- It is cheap
- Biased sample might be chosen if population has a regular pattern which coincides with the sampling interval
- Not completely random

Multistage sampling

is a probability sampling method which involves dividing the population into a number of sub-populations and then selecting a small sample of these sub-populations at random.

Features

- Fewer investigators needed
- Not too costly
- Possibility of bias
- Not truly random method
- Biased sample may result if areas chosen don't reflect full range of the diversity

Cluster sampling

is a non-random sampling method that involves selecting one definable subsection of the population as the sample, that subsection taken to be representative of the population in question.

Features

- Good alternative to multistage sampling if satisfactory sampling frame does not exist
- Inexpensive to operate
- Potential for considerable bias

The only non-probability sampling method that you need to know about for your Business Mathematics studies is quota sampling.

Quota sampling

is a sampling method where randomness is forfeited in the interests of cheapness and administrative simplicity. Investigators are told to interview all the people they meet up to a certain quota.

Features

- Cheap and administratively easy
- No sampling frame
- Much larger samples can be studied
- It can yield enough accurate information for many forms of commercial market research
- May result in certain biases

5: Data presentation

Topic List

Tables and bar charts

Frequency distributions

Histograms

Ogives

Scatter diagrams

Time series graphs

Once raw data has been collected, we need to summarise the data we have collected so that they can be of use. One of the most basic ways of summarising data is the preparation of a table.

Data can also be summarised in a frequency distribution. Bar charts, histograms and ogives are the pictorial representation of grouped and cumulative frequency distributions. Data recorded over time can be presented as time series graphs.

A table is a matrix of data in rows and columns, with the rows and the columns having titles.

TITLE

	Column 1	Column 2	Column 3	Total
Row 1	X	X	X	X
Row 2	X	X	X	X
Row 3	X	X	X	X
Total	X	X	X	X

BEWARE OF PACKING TOO MUCH DATA INTO A TABLE!

Bar charts

are a method of data presentation in which data are represented by bars of equal width, the height/length of the bar corresponding to the value of the data. Axes must be labelled and there must be a scale to indicate the magnitude of the data.

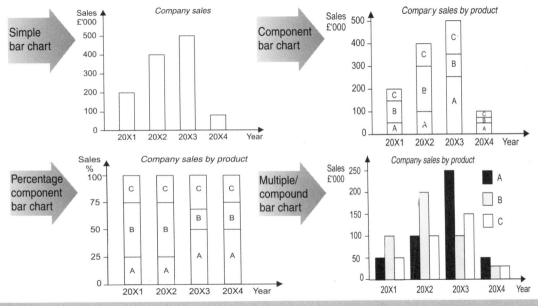

Ungrouped frequency distributions are useful for presenting discrete data.

Grouped frequency distributions are a helpful way of presenting a set of data if each data item has a different value.

Example

Number of brothers and sisters of students on a revision course

Number	Frequency
0	2
1	3
2	4
3	2
4	1
	12

Example

Output of Department A employees in one week

Units of output	Frequency
550 - 599	2
600 - 649	1
650 - 699	4
700 - 749	3
	10

A cumulative frequency distribution or table can be used to show the total number of times that a value above or below a certain amount occurs.

Grouped frequency distributions can also be used to present data for continuous variables.

Example - 'LESS THAN'

Height (cm)	Frequency
≤150	1
≤160	3
≤170	10
≤180	12

Example - 'GREATER THAN'

Height (cm)	Frequency
>0	12
>150	11
>160	9
>170	2

Example

Height (cm)	Frequency
Up to and including 150	1
Over 150, up to and including 160	2
Over 160, up to and including 170	7
Over 170	2
	12

- Can use 'at least ...' also

- Can use 'less than ...' also

Histograms

- Pictorial representation of a frequency distribution

- Usually used when grouped data of a continuous variable are presented but can be used for discrete data by treating the data as continuous (no gaps between class intervals)

- Area covered by bar and not by height represents number of observations in a class

- Width of bar is proportionate to corresponding class interval

- Can be converted into a frequency polygon

- If drawn with very narrow classes, a frequency polygon becomes virtually a curve (a frequency curve)

Method of construction

1 Pick a standard class interval

2 Height of bar (frequency density) = frequency × (standard class interval ÷ actual class interval)

3 Width of bar = actual class interval

4 Width of bar for open-ended classes is the same as that of adjoining class

The graph below shows an histogram and how it can be converted into a frequency polygon.

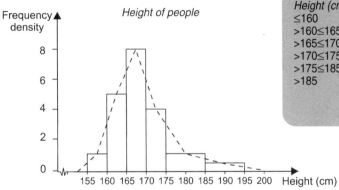

Frequency density

Height of people

Example

Heights of 21 people

Height (cm)	Frequency	Height of bar
≤160	1	$(1 \times 5) \div 5 = 1$
>160≤165	5	$(5 \times 5) \div 5 = 5$
>165≤170	8	$(8 \times 5) \div 5 = 8$
>170≤175	4	$(4 \times 5) \div 5 = 4$
>175≤185	2	$(2 \times 5) \div 10 = 1$
>185	1	$(1 \times 5) \div 10 = \frac{1}{2}$
	$\overline{\underline{21}}$	

Ogives show the cumulative number of items with a value less than or equal to (upward sloping) or greater than or equal to (download sloping) a certain amount.

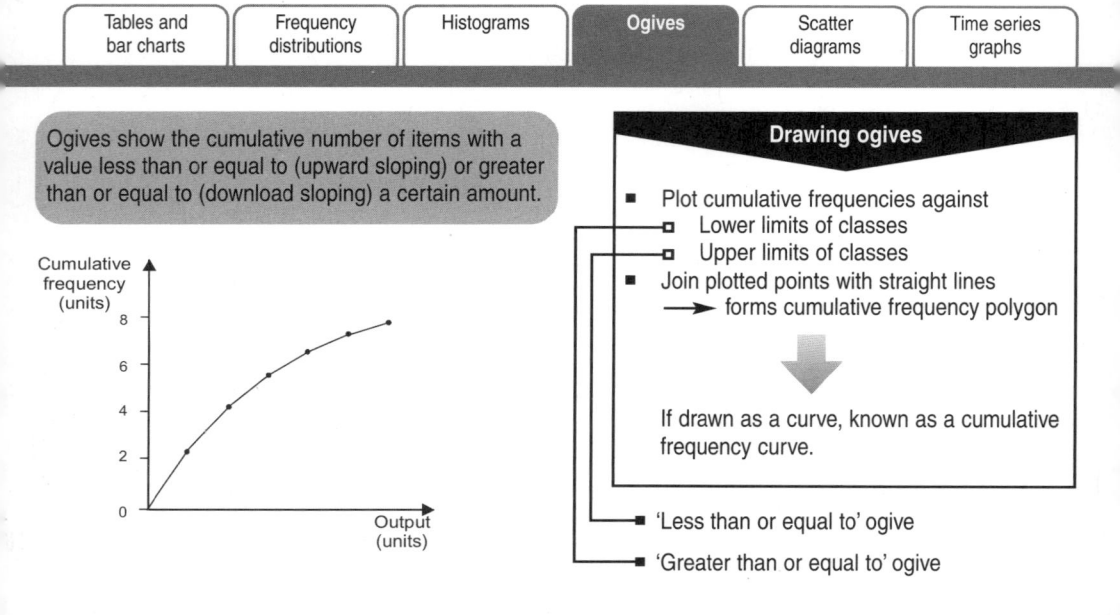

Drawing ogives

- Plot cumulative frequencies against
  - Lower limits of classes
  - Upper limits of classes
- Join plotted points with straight lines
  → forms cumulative frequency polygon

If drawn as a curve, known as a cumulative frequency curve.

- 'Less than or equal to' ogive
- 'Greater than or equal to' ogive

Scatter diagrams are constructed by plotting each pair of data on a graph.

Scatter diagrams are graphs which are used to exhibit data in order to compare the way in which two variables vary with each other.

Features

- x axis represents the independent variable
- y axis represents the dependent variable
- used to identify trend lines and make predictions

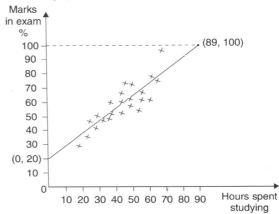

5: Data presentation

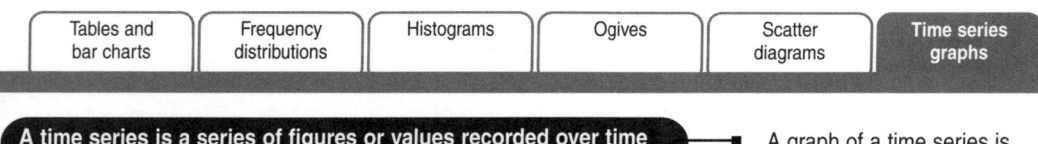

A time series is a series of figures or values recorded over time such as monthly sales over the last two years.

A graph of a time series is known as an historigram.

Features

- Horizontal axis represents time
- Vertical axis represents values of the data recorded
- Graph gives indication of the trend in data over time

EXAM

Remember to draw graphs neatly in an exam. Always use a ruler, label your axes and use an appropriate scale.

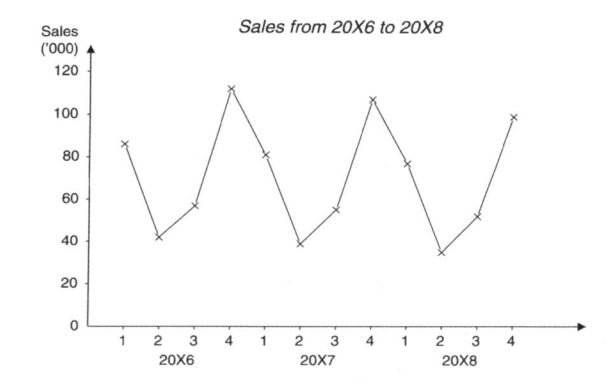

Sales from 20X6 to 20X8

6: Averages

Topic List

Arithmetic mean

Mode

Median

Once data has been collected and presented in a useful form, it needs to be analysed. For example, we might wish to calculate a measure of centrality (average). There are three main types of average.

- Arithmetic mean
- Mode
- Median

An average is a representative figure that is used to give some impression of the size of all the items in the population.

Arithmetic mean	Mode	Median

Ungrouped data	Arithmetic mean	Grouped data
$\bar{x} = \dfrac{\sum x}{n}$	$\bar{x}$	$\bar{x} = \dfrac{\sum fx}{n} = \dfrac{\sum fx}{\sum f}$

Σ = sum of
f = frequency
n = number of items

Formula provided in exam

Formula provided in exam

Advantages

- Widely understood
- It is easy to calculate
- Represents whole set of data
- Suited to further statistical analysis

Disadvantages

- Value may not correspond to an actual value
- Distorted by extreme values

The mode (modal value) is an average which is the most frequently occurring value.

Example

Daily demand for stock in a ten-day period.

Demand	Number of days
Units	
10	4
11	8
12	2

Mode = 11 units because it is the value which occurs most frequently.

Advantages

- Easy to find
- Uninfluenced by a few extreme values
- Can be used for non-numerical data
- Can be value of an actual item in the distribution

Disadvantages

- Ignores dispersion around modal value
- Does not take every value into account
- There can be two or more modes in a data set
- Some instability in the measure

6: Averages

The mode of a grouped frequency distribution can be estimated from a histogram.

Modal class of a histogram is always the class with the tallest bar.

The mode can be estimated graphically as follows.

Step 1. Join with a straight line the top left hand corner of the bar for the modal class and the top left hand corner of the next bar to the right.

Step 2. Join with a straight line the top right hand corner of the bar for the modal class and the top right hand corner of the next bar to the left.

Where these two lines intersect we find the estimated modal value.

Histogram showing mode

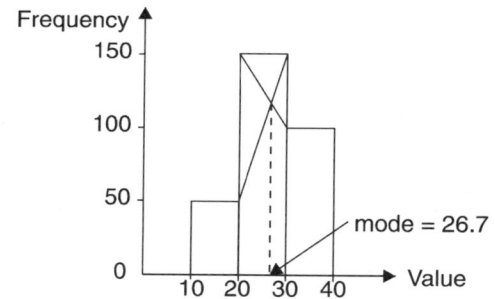

The median is the value of the middle item of a distribution once all of the items have been arranged in order of magnitude.

A list of items in order of value is called an array

Advantages

- Easy to understand
- Unaffected by extreme values
- Can be the value of an actual item in the distribution

Disadvantages

- Fails to reflect the full range of values
- Unsuitable for further statistical analysis
- Producing arrays can be tedious

The middle item of an odd number of items is calculated as

$$\frac{(n + 1)^{th}}{2} \text{ item}$$

The middle item of an even number of items is calculated as

$$\frac{n^{th}}{2} \text{ item}$$

The median of a grouped frequency distribution can be estimated from an ogive.

Example

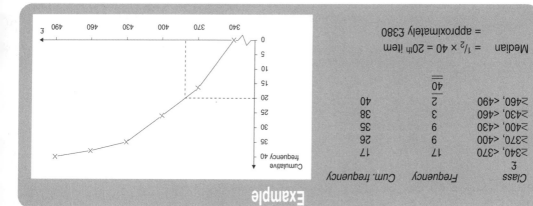

Class £	Frequency	Cum. frequency
≥340, <370	17	17
≥370, <400	9	26
≥400, <430	9	35
≥430, <460	3	38
≥460, <490	2	40
	$\overline{\overline{40}}$	

Median $= \frac{1}{2} \times 40 = 20^{th}$ item
= approximately £380

7: Dispersion

Topic List

We have just revised the first type of statistic that can be used to determine the central point of a distribution - the average. Averages, however, don't give any information about how the values in a distribution are dispersed.

Measures of dispersion give some idea of the spread of a variable about its average.

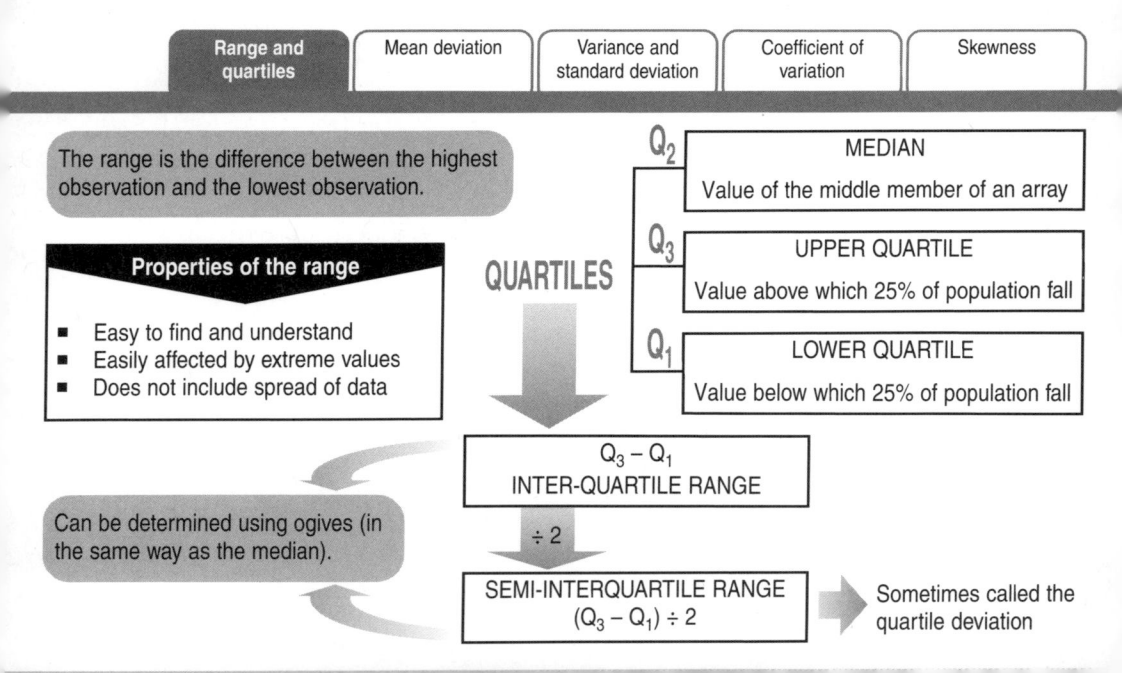

| Range and quartiles | Mean deviation | Variance and standard deviation | Coefficient of variation | Skewness |

The range is the difference between the highest observation and the lowest observation.

Properties of the range

- Easy to find and understand
- Easily affected by extreme values
- Does not include spread of data

Can be determined using ogives (in the same way as the median).

QUARTILES

Q_2 MEDIAN
Value of the middle member of an array

Q_3 UPPER QUARTILE
Value above which 25% of population fall

Q_1 LOWER QUARTILE
Value below which 25% of population fall

$Q_3 - Q_1$
INTER-QUARTILE RANGE

$\div 2$

SEMI-INTERQUARTILE RANGE
$(Q_3 - Q_1) \div 2$

Sometimes called the quartile deviation

The mean deviation is a measure of the average amount by which the values in a distribution (x) differ from the arithmetic mean($\bar{x}$).

You need to learn this formula – it is not provided in the exam

$$\text{Mean deviation} = \frac{\sum f|x - \bar{x}|}{n}$$

Vertical bars mean that all differences are taken as positive

Main properties

- Uses all values in the distribution
- Not greatly affected by extreme values because an average is taken
- Not suitable for further statistical analysis

7: Dispersion

| Range and quartiles | Mean deviation | Variance and standard deviation | Coefficient of variation | Skewness |

The **variance**, σ^2, is the average of the squared mean deviation for each value in a distribution.

Most important measures of spread

The **standard deviation**, σ measures the spread of data around the mean. In general, the larger σ, the more dispersed the data.

Standard deviation = $\sqrt{\text{variance}}$

Properties of the standard deviation

- Uses all values in the distribution
- Suitable for further statistical analysis
- More difficult to understand than other measures of dispersion

CALCULATION OF VARIANCE

Step 1. Difference between value and mean $(x - \overline{x})$

Step 2. Square the difference $(x - \overline{x})^2$

When there are several items together, the following rules apply.

- Arithmetic mean = $n\overline{x}$
- Variance = $n\sigma^2$
- Standard deviation = $\sqrt{n\sigma^2}$

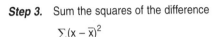

UNGROUPED DATA

Step 3. Sum the squares of the difference

$$\sum (x - \overline{x})^2$$

Step 4. Average of the sum, variance = σ^2

$$\sigma^2 = \frac{\sum (x - \overline{x})^2}{n}$$

$$\sigma = \sqrt{\frac{\sum (x - \overline{x})^2}{n}}$$

$$\sigma = \sqrt{\frac{\sum x^2}{n} - \overline{x}^2}$$

GROUPED DATA

Step 3. Sum the squares of the difference

$$\sum f(x - \overline{x})^2$$

Step 4. Average of the sum, variance = σ^2

$$\sigma^2 = \frac{\sum f(x - \overline{x})^2}{\sum f}$$

$$\sigma = \sqrt{\frac{\sum f(x - \overline{x})^2}{\sum f}}$$

$$\sigma = \sqrt{\frac{\sum f x^2}{\sum f} - \left(\frac{\sum f x}{\sum f}\right)^2}$$

STANDARD DEVIATION

These formulae are provided in the exam

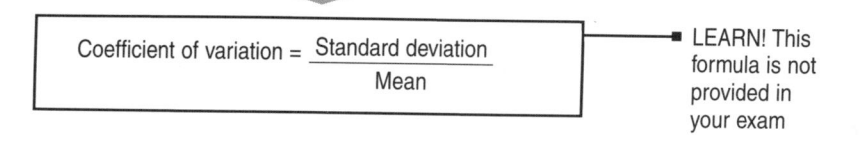

| Range and quartiles | Mean deviation | Variance and standard deviation | **Coefficient of variation** | Skewness |

It is sometimes useful to be able to compare the spreads of two different distributions.

Calculate coefficient of variation (coefficient of relative spread)

$$\text{Coefficient of variation} = \frac{\text{Standard deviation}}{\text{Mean}}$$

■ LEARN! This formula is not provided in your exam

In general, the higher the coefficient of variation, the wider the spread (ie the distribution is more highly dispersed).

Skewness is the asymmetry of a frequency distribution curve.

Negative skewness

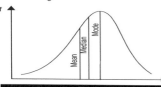

Properties

- Mean, median and mode all different values
- Mode > median
- Mean < median
- Graph leans to right hand side

Symmetrical distribution

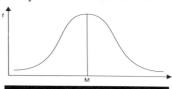

Properties

- Mean = Mode = Median
- Two halves are mirror images of each other

Positive skewness

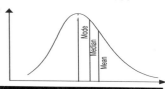

Properties

- Mean, median and mode all different values
- Mode < median
- Mean > median
- Graph leans to left hand side

7: Dispersion

8: Index numbers

Topic List

Index numbers provide a standardised way of comparing the values over time of:

- *Prices*
- *Wages*
- *Volumes*

They are used extensively in business, government and commerce in order to measure performance.

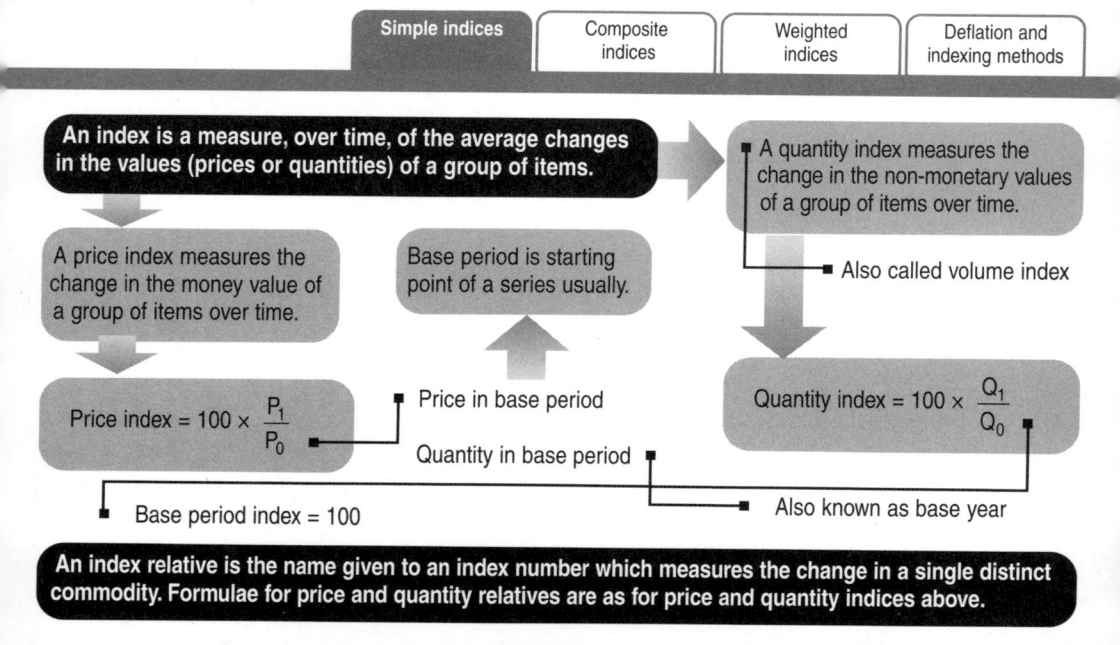

| Simple indices | Composite indices | Weighted indices | Deflation and indexing methods |

An index is a measure, over time, of the average changes in the values (prices or quantities) of a group of items.

A quantity index measures the change in the non-monetary values of a group of items over time.

■ Also called volume index

A price index measures the change in the money value of a group of items over time.

Base period is starting point of a series usually.

Price index = $100 \times \dfrac{P_1}{P_0}$

■ Price in base period

Quantity in base period ■

■ Base period index = 100

Quantity index = $100 \times \dfrac{Q_1}{Q_0}$

■ Also known as base year

An index relative is the name given to an index number which measures the change in a single distinct commodity. Formulae for price and quantity relatives are as for price and quantity indices above.

A composite index number is an index number covering more than one item.

Simple aggregate price index $= \dfrac{\sum P_1}{\sum P_0}$

Average indices

Average price relatives index $= 100 \times \dfrac{1}{n} \times \sum \left(\dfrac{P_1}{P_0} \right)$

Average quantity relatives index $= 100 \times \dfrac{1}{n} \times \sum \left(\dfrac{Q_1}{Q_0} \right)$

Overcome the problem of items being expressed in different units and consider changes in prices and quantities as ratios instead of absolutes

DISADVANTAGES

- Ignores quantities
- Ignores units

Weighting takes account of the relative importance of each item.

WEIGHTED INDEX NUMBERS

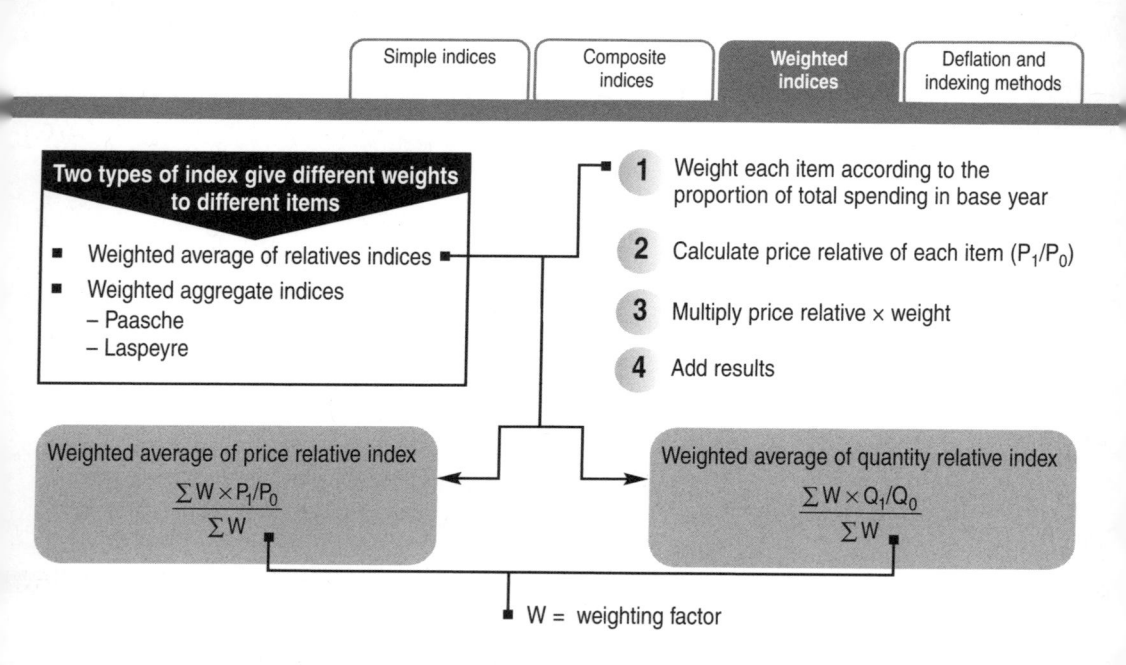

Simple indices | Composite indices | **Weighted indices** | Deflation and indexing methods

Two types of index give different weights to different items

- Weighted average of relatives indices
- Weighted aggregate indices
  - Paasche
  - Laspeyre

1. Weight each item according to the proportion of total spending in base year

2. Calculate price relative of each item (P_1/P_0)

3. Multiply price relative × weight

4. Add results

Weighted average of price relative index

$$\frac{\sum W \times P_1/P_0}{\sum W}$$

Weighted average of quantity relative index

$$\frac{\sum W \times Q_1/Q_0}{\sum W}$$

W = weighting factor

By deflating time-related data using a suitable index, the effects of inflation can be removed. Actual money values ⟶ real (inflation-adjusted) values

$$\text{Real index} = \frac{\text{current value}}{\text{base value}} \times \frac{\text{base indicator}}{\text{current indicator}}$$

Index relatives can be calculated using
- Fixed base method
- Chain base method

FIXED BASE METHOD

A base year is a selected (index 100) and all subsequent changes are measured against this base. This approach should only be used if the basic nature of the commodity is unchanged over time.

CHAIN BASE METHOD

Changes are calculated with respect to the value of the commodity in the period immediately before. This approach can be used for any set of commodity values and must be used if the basic nature of the commodity is changing over time.

8: Index numbers

9: Introduction to probability

Topic List

Laws of probability

Expected values

Expectation and decision making

Probability is a measure of likelihood of an event happening in the long run or over a large number of times. It is stated as a percentage, a ratio, or a number from 0 to 1.

- *Probability = 0 = impossibility*
- *Probability = 1 = certainty*
- *Probability = ½ = 50% chance of happening*
- *Probability = ¼ = 1 in 4 chance of happening*

SIMPLE PROBABILITY

Example

A coin is tossed in the air. What is the probability that it will come down heads?

$$P(\text{heads}) = \frac{\text{Number of ways of achieving desired result (heads)}}{\text{Total number of possible outcomes (heads or tails)}}$$

$$= \frac{1}{2} \text{ or } 50\% \text{ or } 0.5$$

Complementary outcomes

$P(\overline{A}) = 1 - P(A)$ where $\underline{\overline{A}}$ is 'not A'

eg A card is selected from a deck of cards. What is the probability of not getting a ten?

$$P(10) = \frac{4}{52} = \frac{1}{13}$$

$$P(\text{not } 10) = 1 - \frac{1}{13} = \frac{12}{13}$$

Mutually exclusive outcomes

are outcomes where the occurrence of one of the outcomes excludes the possibility of any of the others happening.

Independent events

are events where the outcome of one event in no way affects the outcome of the other events.

Dependent/conditional events

are events where the outcome of one event depends on the outcome of the others.

SIMPLE ADDITION/OR LAW

- $P(A \text{ or } B) = P(A) + P(B)$ where A and B are mutually exclusive outcomes

  This law considers the outcome of one event only.

- This formula is provided in your exam

Example

One card is removed from a deck of cards. What is the probability that it is an ace of spades or a ten?

$P(\text{ace of spades or a ten}) = P(\text{ace of spades}) + P(10)$

$$= \frac{1}{52} + \frac{4}{52}$$

$$= \frac{5}{52}$$

SIMPLE MULTIPLICATION/AND LAW

- $P(A \text{ and } B) = P(A) P(B)$ where A and B are independent events

  This law is used when an event is repeated more than once.

- This formula is provided in your exam

Example

A card is selected from a deck of cards, inspected and replaced. This procedure is repeated. What is the probability that both cards are red?

$P(1^{st} \text{ card red, } 2^{nd} \text{ card red}) = P(1^{st} \text{ card red}) \times P(2^{nd} \text{ card red})$

$= \frac{26}{52} \times \frac{26}{52}$

$= \frac{1}{4}$

GENERAL RULE OF ADDITION

- P(A or B) = P(A) + P(B) – P(A and B)   where A and B are **not** mutually exclusive

This rule considers the outcome of one event.

- This formula is provided in your exam

Example

One card is removed from a deck of cards. What is the probability that it is an ace of spaces or a black card?

P(ace of spades or a black card) = P(ace of spaces) + P(black card) – P(ace of spades *and* a black card)

$$= \frac{1}{52} + \frac{26}{52} - \frac{1}{52}$$

$$= \frac{26}{52}$$

GENERAL RULE OF MULTIPLICATION

$$P(A \text{ and } B) = P(A) \times P(B/A)$$

$$= P(B) \times P(A/B)$$

where A and B are dependent events, the occurrence of the second event being dependent upon the occurrence of the first

- This formula is provided in your exam

Example

Two cards are removed from a deck of cards. What is the probability that they are both red cards?

$P(1^{st} \text{ card red and } 2^{nd} \text{ card red}) = P(1^{st} \text{ card red}) \times P(2^{nd} \text{ card red given that first is a red card})$

$= \frac{26}{52} \times \frac{25}{51}$

$= \frac{25}{102}$

The expected outcome of an event/several events is called the expected value (EV).

If the probability of an outcome is p, then the expected number of times that this outcome will occur in n events (EV) = n × p.

Example

The probability that a component is defective is 0.04. The number of defective components expected in a batch of 2,000 is

$$EV = 2,000 \times 0.04 = 80.$$

If an event occurs many times then, in the long run, the expected value should approximately equal the actual average.

Example

The daily sales of product X may be as follows.

Units	Probability
50	0.2
60	0.8
	1.0

EV of daily sales = (50 × 0.2) + (60 × 0.8) = 58

In the long run the actual average daily sales of product X should be 58 units.

9: Introduction to probability

An expected value can be calculated when an event will only occur once or twice, but it will not be a true long-run average of what will actually happen because there is no long run.

Example

A project has two possible outcomes:

Profit/loss	Probability
£	
40,000	0.3
(5,000)	0.7

EV of profit = (40,000 × 0.3) + ((5,000) × 0.7) = £8,500

The concepts of probability and expected value are vital in business decision making. The expected values for single events can offer a helpful guide for management decisions.

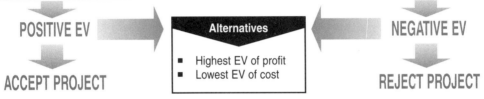

POSITIVE EV ➔ **ACCEPT PROJECT**

Alternatives
- Highest EV of profit
- Lowest EV of cost

NEGATIVE EV ➔ **REJECT PROJECT**

Use of payoff tables

If a decision has a range of possible actions ⟶ columns of table
and if each action will have certain consequences (payoffs) ⟶ cells of table
which will depend on circumstances ⟶ rows of table not dependent on the action taken.

Example

Selling price per unit = £12   Cost per unit = £7

Possible demand: 100 units (30% probability)
                  200 units (70% probability)

Actions: Produce either 100 or 200 units

Production levels
                  100   200
Demand   100   100   200
         200   500   500   *(100 × 12) − (200 × 7)
         1,000   500   200

Expected contribution (100 produced) = (£500 × 30%) + (£500 × 70%) = £500

Expected contribution (200 produced) = (£200 × 30%) + (£1,000 × 70%) = £640

Therefore produce 200 units because expected contribution higher.

10: The normal distribution

Topic List

The normal distribution is a type of probability distribution. Probability distributions analyse the proportion of times a particular value occurs in a set of items. Probability distributions also provide a method of arriving at the probability of an event without having to go through all the probability rules that we looked at in Chapter 9.

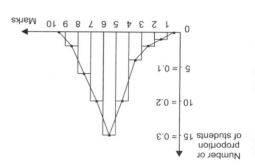

The graph of a probability distribution is the same as that of a frequency distribution but with the vertical axis marked in proportions rather than numbers.

The area under a curve in a probability distribution is 100% or 1 (the total of all probabilities).

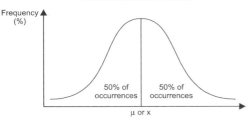

Normal distribution curve

Frequency (%)

50% of occurrences | 50% of occurrences

μ or x

Properties

- Area under curve totals exactly 1

- It is symmetrical

- The mean $= \mu$

- Area to the left of μ = area to the right of μ = 0.5

- 68% of frequencies occur in the range mean $\pm$ 1 standard deviation

- 95% of frequencies occur in the range mean $\pm$ 1.96 standard deviations

- 99% of frequencies occur in the range mean $\pm$ 2.58 standard deviations

There are an infinite number of normal distributions.

Each different distribution depends on the value of μ and σ.

The relative spread of frequencies around the mean is the same for all normal distributions

NORMAL DISTRIBUTION TABLES

These give the proportion of the total which is between the mean μ and a point x which is z standard deviations above the mean.

$$z = \frac{x - \mu}{\sigma}$$

■ This formula is provided in your exam. Make sure you know how to use it correctly.

Example

If x = 100, μ = 200 and σ = 50

Identify the z score and the corresponding proportion using normal distribution tables.

$$z = \frac{x - \mu}{\sigma}$$

$$= \frac{100 - 200}{50}$$

$$= 2$$

A z score of 2 corresponds to a proportion of 0.4772 or 47.72%.

Example

If z = 1.96, what does this mean?

From normal distribution tables, 1.96 corresponds to an area of 0.4750 or 47.5%.

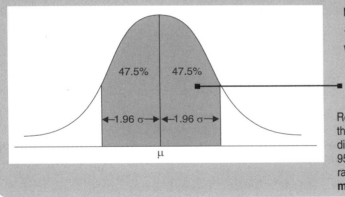

Normal distribution is symmetrical.

1.96σ above and below the mean will correspond to the same area.

Total shaded area = 47.5% × 2
= 95%

Remember how we stated earlier in this chapter that one of the normal distribution's properties was that 95% of frequencies occur in the range

mean ± 1.96 standard deviations.

The normal distribution is a type of probability distribution and can therefore be used to calculate probabilities

In an exam make sure that you always draw a sketch of a normal distribution to identify the areas that you are interested in when using the normal distribution to calculate probabilities.

Example

The daily wage rate of employees in an industry are normally distributed with a mean of £200 and a standard deviation of £20.

What proportion of employees earn between £160 to £220 per day?

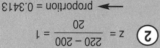

① $z = \dfrac{160 - 200}{20} = 2$ ← proportion = 0.4772

② $z = \dfrac{220 - 200}{20} = 1$ ← proportion = 0.3413

Proportion of employees earning £160 – £220 per day = 0.4772 + 0.3413 = 0.8185

Alternatively, probability of an employee earning £160 – £220 per day = 81.85%

11: Interest

Topic List

Simple and compound interest

Regular investments

Regular repayments

If a company or an individual puts some capital into an investment, a financial return will be expected.

When you invest your savings in a building society account, you expect your money to grow (or compound) over time. This chapter looks at how to calculate financial returns and also the cost of borrowing money (mortgages and loans).

Simple interest

is interest which is earned in equal amounts each period and which is a given proportion of the original investment (principal).

Compound interest

is interest which, as it is earned, is added to the original investment and earns interest itself.

where X = original sum invested
r = interest rate (as a proportion)
n = number of periods
S = sum invested after n periods (future value)

$$S = X + nrX$$

$$S = X(1 + r)^n$$

Calculate NBV of an asset using reducing balance method of depreciation by applying a negative interest rate

If r changes during the period of an investment, the formula becomes: $S = X(1 + r_1)^y (1 + r_2)^{n-y}$
Where y = the period of time for which the initial interest rate, r_1 applies and $n - y$ = the (balancing) period of time for which the next rate of interest, r_2, applies.

The final (terminal) value of an investment to which equal annual amounts are added = S

$$S = \frac{A(R^n - 1)}{R - 1}$$

where
- A = the first term
- R = the common ratio
- n = the number of terms

Sinking fund

is an investment into which equal annual instalments are paid in order to earn interest, so that by the end of a given number of years, the investment is large enough to pay off a known commitment at that time.

An individual may make annual payments into a pension fund or monthly savings into a building society savings account. You might be asked to calculate the future (terminal) value of an investment to which equal annual amounts will be added.

Example

Sinking fund to replace an asset in three years' time. Value of fund must be £50,000. Fund will earn interest at 10%.

$$S = £50,000 = \frac{A \times (1.1^3 - 1)}{1.1 - 1}$$

$$A = \frac{£50,000 \times 0.1}{1.1^3 - 1} = £15,106$$

11: Interest

Loan repayments (for example repayment mortgage) can be calculated using the formula for the sum of a geometric progression. The sum of the repayments (S) must equal the final value of the loan (mortgage).

$$S = \frac{A(R^n - 1)}{R - 1}$$

Example

Tilly has taken out a £30,000 mortgage over 25 years. Interest is charged at 12%. What is the monthly repayment?

Final value of mortgage $= £30,000 \times (1.12)^{25}$
$= £510,002$

Sum of repayments, S $= \dfrac{A((1.12)^{25} - 1)}{1.12 - 1}$
$= 133.334A$

Sum of repayments = final value of mortgage

$133.334A = £510,002$

$A = £510,002 \div 133.334 = £3,825$

Monthly repayment $= £3,825 \div 12 = £318.75$

Nominal rate = interest rate as a per annum figure

Adjusted nominal rate = equivalent annual rate

Equivalent annual rate = effective annual rate

Effective annual rate = annual percentage rate (APR) = Compound annual rate (CAR)

12: Discounting

Topic List

Concept of discounting

Net Present Value Method

Internal Rate of Return Method

NPV versus IRR

Annuities and perpetuities

Discounting is the reverse of compounding. Its major application in business is in the evaluation of investments, to decide whether they offer a satisfactory return to the investor. There are two main methods of using discounting to appraise investments.

- *Net Present Value (NPV) Method*
- *Internal Rate of Return (IRR) Method*

The basic principle of discounting is that if we wish to have £S in a year's time, we need to invest a certain sum now (year 0) at the interest rate of r% in order to obtain the required sum of money in the future.

Discounting formula

Present value, $X = S \times \dfrac{1}{(1+r)^n}$

Discount factors are shown in present value tables provided in the exam.

Example

What is the PV of £100,000 received in five years' time if r = 6% per annum?

$$X = S \times \frac{1}{(1+r)^n}$$

$$= £100,000 \times \frac{1}{(1+0.06)^5}$$

$$= £74,726$$

Net Present Value Method

Work out present values of all cashflows (income and expenditure) related to an investment

- Positive NPV – accept investment
- Negative NPV – reject investment
- If two or more projects are viable, rank them in order of highest NPV per £ invested

Work out a net total (NPV)

Example

Year	Cashflow	Discount factor	Present value
	£	10%	£
0	(10,000)	1.000	(10,000)
1	1,000	0.909	909
2-4*	10,000	2.261	22,610
		NPV →	13,519

Cashflows spread over a year are assumed to occur at the year end

'Now' is the last day of year 0

IRR method of discounted cashflow

This method determines the rate of interest (internal rate of return) at which the NPV is 0 (the investment's rate of return).

Graphical

Sketch a graph of NPV against discounted rate.

Find the point where the curve crosses the x-axis (ie where NPV = zero)

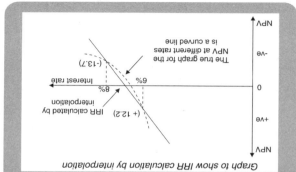

Graph to show IRR calculation by interpolation

Interpolation

$$IRR = a\% + \left[\frac{A}{A-B} \times (b-a) \right] \%$$

where
a = one interest rate
b = the other interest rate
A = NPV at rate A
B = NPV at rate B

This formula is **not** provided in your exam – you must learn it!

Sometimes there will be conflict between the NPV and IRR methods of investment appraisal.

Advantages of IRR method

- The information it provides is more easily understood by managers, especially non-financial managers

- A discount rate does not have to be specified before the IRR can be calculated. A given cost of capital rate is simply required to which the IRR can be compared

Advantages of NPV method

- This method takes into account the relative size of investments (unlike the IRR method)

- When discount rates are expected to differ over the life of a project, such variations can be incorporated easily into NPV calculations, but not into IRR calculations

Annuity

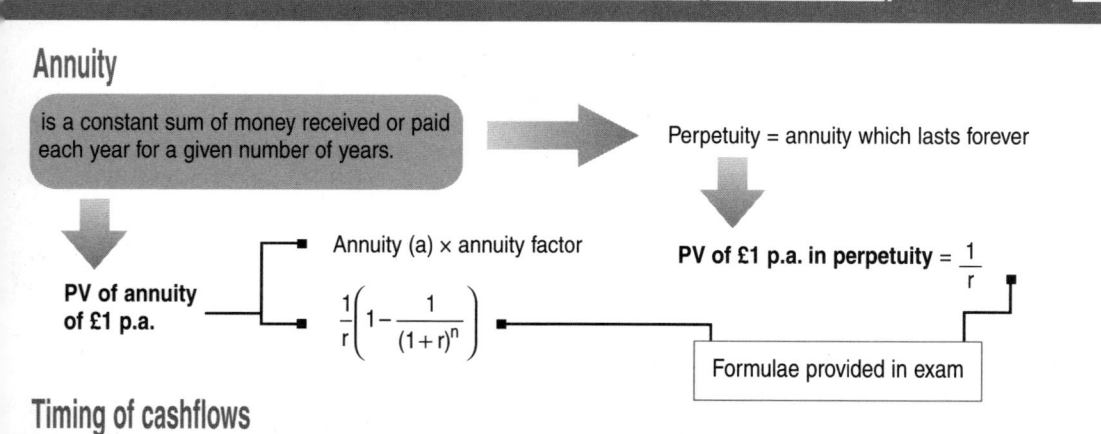

is a constant sum of money received or paid each year for a given number of years.

Perpetuity = annuity which lasts forever

PV of annuity of £1 p.a.

Annuity (a) × annuity factor

$$\frac{1}{r}\left(1 - \frac{1}{(1+r)^n}\right)$$

PV of £1 p.a. in perpetuity $= \frac{1}{r}$

Formulae provided in exam

Timing of cashflows

Note that both cumulative present value tables and the formulae assume that the first payment or receipt is **a year from now**. For example, if there are five equal payments starting now, and the interest rate is 8%, we should use a factor of 1 (for today's payment) plus 3.312 (for the other four payments) = 4.312.

13: Time series analysis

Topic List

Finding the trend

Finding the seasonal variations

Forecasting and time series analysis

A time series is a series of figures or values recorded over time such as output at a factory each day for a month. The graph of a time series is called a historigram.

Each time series is made up of a combination of four components.

- *Trend*
- *Seasonal variations*
- *Cyclical variations*
- *Random variations*

Three main methods of finding a trend
- Line of best fit (trend line)
- Linear regression (least squares method)
- Moving averages

The moving averages method attempts to remove seasonal variations from actual data by the process of averaging, in order to identify the trend.

The additive model

$$Y = T + S + I$$

The multiplicative model

$$Y = T \times S \times I$$

where
- Y = actual time series
- T = trend series
- S = seasonal component
- I = random component

Moving averages – odd number of periods

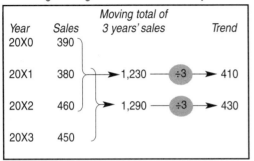

Year	Sales	Moving total of 3 years' sales		Trend
20X0	390			
20X1	380	→ 1,230 → ÷3 →		410
20X2	460	→ 1,290 → ÷3 →		430
20X3	450			

Moving averages – even number of periods

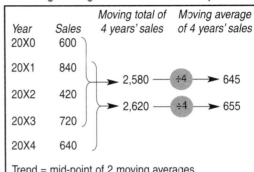

Year	Sales	Moving total of 4 years' sales	Moving average of 4 years' sales
20X0	600		
20X1	840	→ 2,580 → ÷4 →	645
20X2	420	→ 2,620 → ÷4 →	655
20X3	720		
20X4	640		

Trend = mid-point of 2 moving averages
= (645 + 655) ÷ 2 = 650

The seasonal variation can be found using the additive or multiplicative model and by assuming that I, random variations are relatively small.

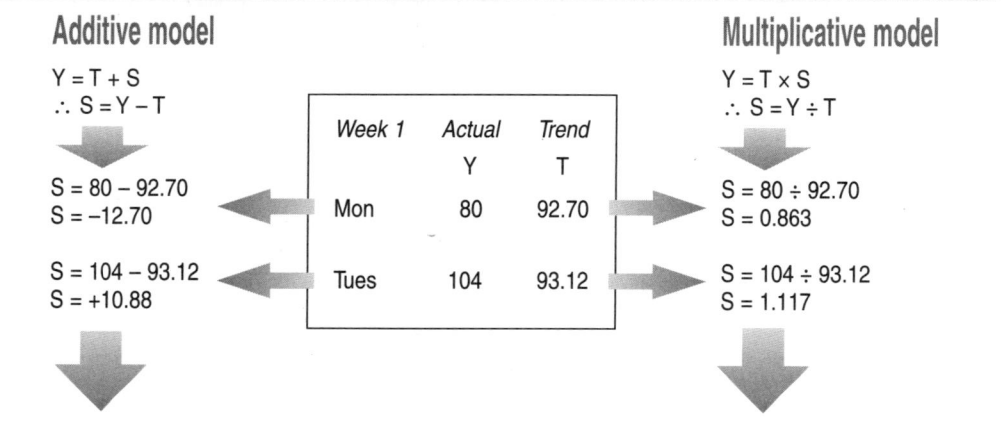

Additive model

$Y = T + S$
$\therefore S = Y - T$

$S = 80 - 92.70$
$S = -12.70$

$S = 104 - 93.12$
$S = +10.88$

Week 1	Actual	Trend
	Y	T
Mon	80	92.70
Tues	104	93.12

Multiplicative model

$Y = T \times S$
$\therefore S = Y \div T$

$S = 80 \div 92.70$
$S = 0.863$

$S = 104 \div 93.12$
$S = 1.117$

Additive

	Mon	Tues
Week 1	−12.70	+10.88
Week 2	−12.80	+14.78
	−25.50	+25.66
Average	−12.75	+12.83

Take an average of seasonal variations

Multiplicative

	Mon	Tues
Week 1	0.863	1.117
Week 2	0.865	1.155
	1.728	2.272
Average	0.864	1.136

Adjust total of seasonal variations

SUM TO ZERO

	Mon	Tues	Wed	Thurs	Fri	Total
Average	−12.75	12.83	0.91	27.49	−32.43	−3.95
Adjust*	+0.79	+0.79	+0.79	+0.79	+0.79	+3.95
Estimate	−11.96	13.62	1.70	28.28	−31.64	0
Round to	-12	14	2	28	−32	

* 3.95 ÷ 5 = 0.79 (additive)

1X NUMBER ITEMS IN CYCLE

	Mon	Tues	Wed	Thurs	Fri	Total
Average	0.8640	1.1360	1.0100	1.2890	0.6600	4.959
Adjust**	0.0082	0.0082	0.0082	0.0082	0.0082	0.041
Estimate	0.8722	1.1442	1.0182	1.2972	0.6682	5.000
Round to	0.87	1.14	1.02	1.30	0.67	

** 0.041 ÷ 5 = 0.0082 (multiplicative)

Time series analysis data can be used to make forecasts as follows.

Step 1. Plot a trend line (line of best fit/moving averages method)

Step 2. Extrapolate the trend line (extend trend line outside range of known data)

Step 3. Adjust forecast trends to obtain actual forecast
- Additive model (add **positive** variations/subtract **negative** variations)
- Multiplicative model (multiply forecast trends by seasonal variations)

Example

Week 4	Trend line readings	Seasonal variations	Forecast
Monday	100.5	−13	87.5
Tuesday	101.1	+16	117.1
Wednesday	101.7	+1	102.7
Thursday	102.2	+28	130.2
Friday	102.8	−32	70.8

14: Correlation and regression

Topic List

Correlation

Coefficient of determination

Spearman's rank correlation coefficient

Estimating the line of best fit

Correlation and regression is a very important topic which forms part of the forecasting section of the syllabus. If we assume that there is a linear relationship between two variables we can determine the equation of a straight line to represent the relationship between the variables and use that equation to make forecasts and predictions.

Correlation

is the extent to which the value of a dependent variable is related to the value of the independent variable.

Degrees of correlation

- Perfectly correlated
- Partly correlated
- Uncorrelated

EXAM FORMULA

Correlation coefficient, $r = \dfrac{n\sum XY - \sum X \sum Y}{\sqrt{[n\sum X^2 - (\sum X)^2][n\sum Y^2 - (\sum Y)^2]}}$

THIS FORMULA WILL BE PROVIDED IN YOUR EXAM

Values of r

- $r = +1$ = perfect positive
- $r = -1$ = perfect negative
- $r = 0$ = uncorrelated

Coefficient of determination, r^2

r^2 measures the proportion of the total variation in the value of one variable that can be explained by variations in the value of the other variable.

If $r = 0.9$, $r^2 = 0.81$

If the correlation coefficient of two variables $= 0.9$, we know the variables are **positively correlated**. The coefficient of determination, $r^2 = 0.81$ and this gives a more meaningful analysis. We know that 81% of the variations in the value of y **could** be explained by variations in the value of x.

Note: we do not conclude that 81% of variations in y are caused by variations in x. We say that 81% of variations in y can be explained by variations in x.

Spearman's rank correlation coefficient, R is used when data is given in terms of order or rank rather than actual values.

■ FORMULA PROVIDED IN EXAM

$$R = 1 - \left[\frac{6\sum d^2}{n(n^2 - 1)} \right]$$

n = number of pairs of data

d = difference between the ranking in each set of data

R is interpreted in the same way as r (the ordinary correlation coefficient) ⟶ values range from −1 to +1.

If items tie a particular ranking (say 3 items for 4th place), an average must be calculated ((4 + 5 + 6) ÷ 3) = 5th place.

Estimating the line of best fit, Y = a + bX (linear relationship)

Scattergraph method (draw a graph)

- Plot pairs of data for related variables

- Produce a scattergraph

- Use judgement to draw line of best fit

- Fixed costs = intersection of line on y axis (a)

- Variable cost per unit = gradient of line (b)

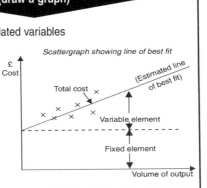

Scattergraph showing line of best fit

£ Cost

(Estimated line of best fit)

Total cost ×

Variable element

Fixed element

Volume of output

Linear regression analysis (mathematical calculation)

- $b = \dfrac{n\sum XY - \sum X \sum Y}{n\sum X^2 - (\sum X)^2}$

- $a = \overline{Y} - b\overline{X}$

- n = number of pairs of data

- $\overline{X}$ = average X value

- $\overline{Y}$ = average Y value

These formulae are provided in your exam

Notes

Notes

Notes

Notes

Notes

Notes

Notes

Notes